FARM ANIMALS

HORSES

by Sheri Doyle

Consulting Editor: Gail Saunders-Smith, PhD

Consultant: Dr. Celina Johnson, College of Agriculture
California State University, Chico

CAPSTONE PRESS
a capstone imprint

Pebble Plus is published by Capstone Press,
1710 Roe Crest Drive, North Mankato, Minnesota 56003.
www.capstonepub.com

Library of Congress Cataloging-in-Publication Data
Doyle, Sheri.
Horses / by Sheri Doyle.
p. cm.—(Pebble plus. Farm animals)
Summary: "Simple text and full-color photographs provide a brief introduction to horses"—Provided by publisher.
ISBN 978-1-4296-8648-8 (library binding)
ISBN 978-1-62065-302-9 (ebook PDF)
1. Horses—Juvenile literature. I. Title.
SF302.D69 2013
636.1—dc23

2011049979

Editorial Credits
Erika L. Shores, editor; Ashlee Suker, designer; Marcie Spence, media researcher; Eric Manske, production specialist

Photo Credits
Alamy: Forget Patrick/sagaphoto.com, 17, Wildlife GmbH, 21; Shutterstock: 1000 Words, 11, anastasija Popova, 9,
angelshot, 7, Cheryl Ann Quigley, 19, CTatiana, cover, 1, lebanman, 13, Lenkadan, 15, Olga_i, 5

Note to Parents and Teachers

The Farm Animals series supports national science standards related to life science.
This book describes and illustrates horses. The images support early readers in understanding
the text. The repetition of words and phrases helps early readers learn new words. This book
also introduces early readers to subject-specific vocabulary words, which are defined in the
Glossary section. Early readers may need assistance to read some words and to use the Table
of Contents, Glossary, Read More, Internet Sites, and Index sections of the book.

Printed in the United States of America in North Mankato, Minnesota.
042012   006682CGF12

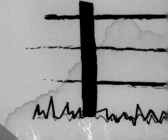

Table of Contents

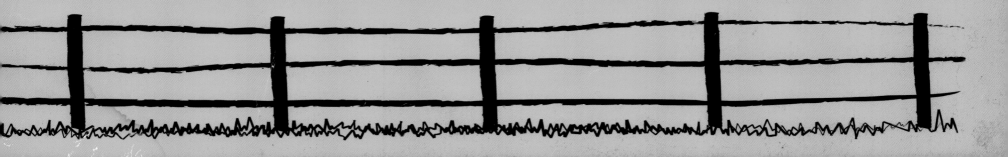

Meet the Horses

Neigh! The sun rises over
the field. Here come some horses!
They gallop with their strong legs.
Their hooves beat the ground.

Horses have wide-set eyes,

pointed ears, and large nostrils.

Horses see, hear, and smell

very well.

Horses can be bay, black, gray, or many other colors. A gold-colored horse is called a palomino. Horses might have spots or other markings.

Horses are measured from the
ground to their shoulders.
The biggest horses can be taller
than 6 feet (1.8 meters).
That's taller than a minivan!

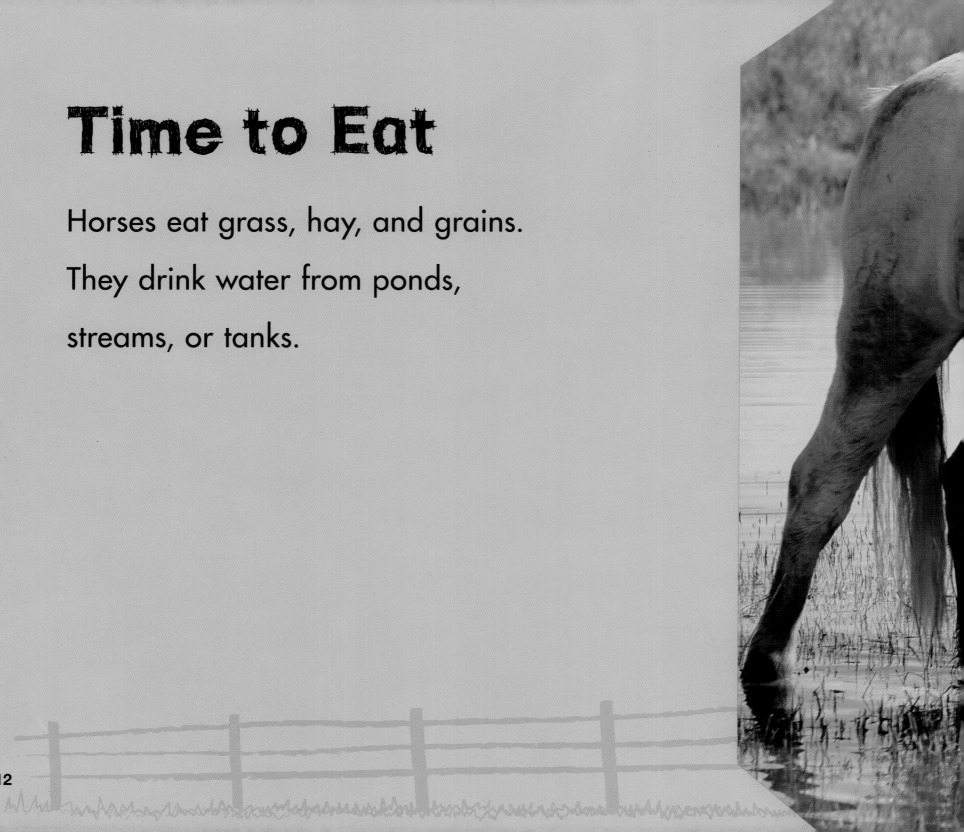

Time to Eat

Horses eat grass, hay, and grains.

They drink water from ponds,

streams, or tanks.

New Life

A foal is born! It stands up just hours after birth. Females grow up to be mares. Males are called geldings or stallions.

Horses can live for 30 years.

Horses in Action

People raise horses for many reasons.

Draft horses, such as Percherons,

can pull heavy loads.

American Quarter horses help

move cattle on ranches.

People ride horses in races,

in shows, and on trails.

Thoroughbreds are fast racehorses.

Arabians are best

for long-distance trail riding.

Time to Rest

Some horses sleep in fenced pastures.

Other horses rest in stalls

inside stables or barns.

Stall floors are padded with straw

or sawdust for a soft bed.

Glossary

bay—brown with a black mane and tail

cattle—a group of cows raised for their meat

foal—a young horse

gallop—the fastest movement or run of a horse

gelding—a male horse that can't be used for breeding

grain—foods like barley, corn, oats, and bran

hoof—the hard part of a horse's foot

mare—a female horse after she turns 4 years old

nostril—an opening in the nose

pasture—land where farm animals eat grass and exercise

show—a contest with many events

stall—a small room inside of a stable or barn

stallion—an adult male horse

Read More

Nelson, Robin. *Horses.* Farm Animals. Minneapolis: Lerner Publications, 2009.

Pitts, Zachary. *The Pebble First Guide to Horses.* Pebble First Guides. Mankato, Minn.: Capstone Press, 2009.

Twine, Alice. *Horses.* Baby Animals. New York: PowerKids Press, 2008.

Internet Sites

FactHound offers a safe, fun way to find Internet sites related to this book. All of the sites on FactHound have been researched by our staff.

Here's all you do:

Visit *www.facthound.com*

Type in this code: 9781429686488

Super-cool stuff! Check out projects, games and lots more at
www.capstonekids.com

Index

Word Count: 201
Grade: 1
Early-Intervention Level: 16